Love to Quilt...

D0719765

Dresden Plates

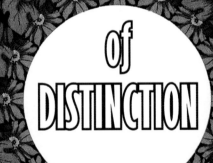

of
DISTINCTION

SHARON
STROUD

American Quilter's Society

P. O. Box 3290 • Paducah, KY 42002-3290
www.AQSquilt.com

Located in Paducah, Kentucky, the American Quilter's Society (AQS) is dedicated to promoting the accomplishments of today's quilters. Through its publications and events, AQS strives to honor today's quiltmakers and their work and to inspire future creativity and innovation in quiltmaking.

Editor: Barbara Smith
Graphic Design: Lisa M. Clark
Cover Design: Michael Buckingham
Photography: Charles R. Lynch

Library of Congress Cataloging-in-Publication Data
Stroud, Sharon.
  Love to quilt : Dresden plates of distinction / by Sharon Stroud.
    p. cm.
  ISBN 1-57432-773-9
  1. Quilting--Patterns.   2. Patchwork--Patterns.   I. Title.
  TT835 .S746 2001
    746.46'041--dc21

                               2001005163

Additional copies of this book may be ordered from the American Quilter's Society, PO Box 3290, Paducah, KY 42002-3290, or online at www.AQSquilt.com.

This book is dedicated...
to two extraordinary women – my maternal grandmother, Elveda May Beardsley Basl, and my maternal great-grandmother, Winifred Fowler Beardsley;

to my parents, Otto and Betty Ann Basl Sperger, who always told me that I could do anything I set my mind to and who supported my decisions;

and to my husband, Floyd Stroud, without whose love and encouragement this book would still be a dream.

I am thankful for each of you and love you all.

Four generations of Sharon's family on her mother's side: (left to right) mother, great grandmother (with her arms around Sharon), grandmother.

Acknowledgments

"No one is an island" is an apt description for life, but never more so than when one is writing a book. Many thanks to all who asked about progress and offered help as the deadline approached.

Special thanks go to the following people:

The Four Seasons group, Debbie Woodard, Shirley Steimle, Linda Ruede, Cindy Miller, and Betty Sperger for encouragement and for always being ready for an impromptu show-and-tell of my latest Dresden Plate quilts.

The late Carol Benson for encouraging me to design and teach my own projects.

The shop owners who give me a venue for classes: Judi West of Patchwork Plus in Skaneateles, New York; Katie Barnaby, Sherry Haefele, Cyndi Slothower, Linda Van Nederynen and Merrie Wilent of Quilters Corner, Ithaca, New York; and Clara Travis of Patchwork and Pies, McLean, New York.

The "Sharon Groupies" (they coined the phrase), who continue to take classes, increasing their skills and allowing me to enjoy the camaraderie and friendship that on-going relationships provide.

Joyce Janowski, Gina Castro, and Debbie Woodard for sharing their quilts and for their special help.

Cathy Bush and Sandy Forrest for also sharing quilts.

Anita Shackelford – friend, mentor, and colleague – for answering endless questions, giving good advice, and contributing the quilt HOME MADE CHRISTMAS for the photo gallery.

My editor, Barbara Smith, who made the whole process easier.

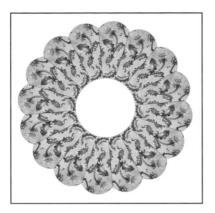

Introduction 6

General Instructions 7

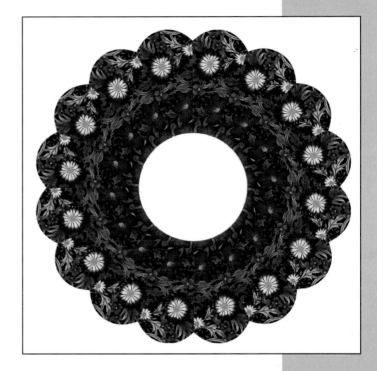

Introduction

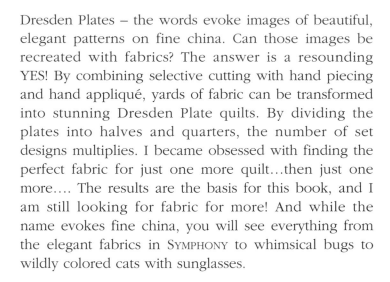

Dresden Plates – the words evoke images of beautiful, elegant patterns on fine china. Can those images be recreated with fabrics? The answer is a resounding YES! By combining selective cutting with hand piecing and hand appliqué, yards of fabric can be transformed into stunning Dresden Plate quilts. By dividing the plates into halves and quarters, the number of set designs multiplies. I became obsessed with finding the perfect fabric for just one more quilt…then just one more…. The results are the basis for this book, and I am still looking for fabric for more! And while the name evokes fine china, you will see everything from the elegant fabrics in SYMPHONY to whimsical bugs to wildly colored cats with sunglasses.

Selective cutting takes more time, but the results will be readily apparent. For those of you who prefer to piece by machine, directions are given, but do give the hand piecing a try. You will be pleasantly surprised at how much you can get done in found bits of time, and you can sit with family and friends and be sociable at the same time. Hand sewing is a wonderful respite from the frenetic pace of life, and it has proven health benefits.

As you peruse these pages, I hope that you will be inspired to make the quilts – from choosing fabric, through the cutting and piecing, the appliqué, the quilting, and the binding. Enjoy each step of the process, and at the end, you can proudly say, "I did the whole thing myself, start to finish." There is certainly nothing wrong with finishing a top and having someone else do the quilting, but nothing can compare with the sense of pride and accomplishment that comes from doing it all.

Read through the book, buy a spectacular fabric, and begin, but be forewarned. These quilts are addicting. Bet you can't make just one.

Always in stitches,

Sharon

CHAPTER ONE

General Instructions

Choosing Fabrics

While there is no set formula for choosing a Dresden Plate fabric, there are certain characteristics to look for. The quilt photos will give you an idea of the range of fabrics that can be used.

Make a plastic window template from the blade pattern on page 70 to carry shopping with you. By moving the template over a fabric, you can tell immediately if it has the size and variety of motifs you want.

Fabrics that have medium-scale prints with frequent color and motif changes are excellent candidates. If the print is too small or uniform, all the plates will look the same. As an example, the dandelion fabric used in GRANDMA BASL LOVED DANDELIONS (page 52) presented an excellent motif size, but almost all the selections would have looked the same when cut and pieced. My decision was to find one outstanding motif and make just one plate. This is an excellent way to showcase a favorite fabric, but more than one plate would have negated the impact. The fabric in SYMPHONY (page 25), on the other hand, had so many possibilities that it was easy to cut the equivalent of 12 plates.

A large-scale print will make more impressionistic plates. Large flowers will not fit entirely into a blade, so the edges will blur together. I like working with a scale of print that allows me to use at least one entire image in a blade. Try both ideas and see which you like better.

You can tell when you have found a great fabric because you start making excited exclamations. People are amused to see me choose fabrics. I'm pretty quiet until I find just the right one; then, as I start moving the template over the yardage, I make oohing and aahing sounds. Everyone laughs because I am so excited, but part of the fun is finding that one fabric that "speaks" to me. I know there is one (or more) out there whispering your name. Can you hear it?

Plate Yardage

Because each fabric is different, specific yardage cannot be given in the patterns. Here is an easy way to determine how much fabric to buy for the plates:

Fig. 1–1: The design repeat for this fabric is 8".

Unfold the fabric. Find an easily recognizable motif. Then look along the fold for the next occurrence. Measure the distance between the two motifs, which is the length of the repeat. For example, in Fig. 1–1, the repeat is 8".

Now, count the number of repeated motifs within that distance. Do not count partial motifs or those too near the selvages, which may be distorted. You will need 16 repeats of the same motif for a whole plate. If there are five motifs every 8", you would calculate as follows:

Example
16 repeats needed ÷ 5 repeated motifs =
3.2 or 4 repeats (rounded up),
4 repeats x 8" = 32" or 1 yard (rounded up).

I round the inches of fabric up to the nearest quarter yard; that is, 8" to ¼ yard, 11" to ½ yard, etc. Rounding up builds in a bit of extra fabric, but because some motifs may be situated near others you want to cut, I suggest buying ½ to 1 yard extra. It's good insurance against running short with one blade left to cut.

The larger the project, the more fabric I buy and the more extra I add. For example, the SYMPHONY quilt (page 25) took more than four yards just for the plates, even though the motifs were repeated eight times per quarter yard.

If you cut your yardage too close, you will have to settle for what you can cut from the last bits of fabric instead of making the last plate as special as the rest. That is what happened in FINE CHINA (page 34). I had 1 yard of fabric. I cut the three rose-colored plates, then had to settle for the predominantly blue fourth. My husband suggested I call this quilt "There's One in Every Crowd." Extra yardage would have given me the choice of either cutting a fourth rose plate or two blue ones to balance the quilt a bit better. I still love it. There is something to be said for serendipity!

Remember that this yardage is for the plates only and does not include the borders. Refer to the project you are making for background and border yardages.

Preparing Fabrics

Wash your fabric in warm water with soap, and machine dry it. Washing fabric will remove the sizing, reduce further shrinkage, and remove excess dye from darker fabrics. Press with a steam iron set on cotton to remove wrinkles. Do not press a new center fold. You will be cutting motifs across the entire piece of fabric, and a fold line will distort the blades.

Supply List

For piecing and appliquéing the plates, you will need the following supplies:

Scissors: Buy large, sharp ones for cutting fabric.

Marking pencils: I prefer soapstone and fine-lead pencils in white, silver, rose, and canary. A mechanical pencil with fine lead is useful for marking seam lines.

Ruler with ¼" markings: The 1" x 6" ruler is handy for trimming.

15" square ruler: This size is handy for cutting blocks.

Rotary cutter and mat

Template plastic

Needles: I prefer sharps, size 10, for both appliqué and piecing, but you may want to try straw (milliner's) needles.

Thread: My preference is 100-percent cotton thread for piecing and appliqué. Match the color to the background of the blade fabric for piecing. Appliqué thread needs to match the color of the outer rim of the plate, or you can choose a neutral color if the color changes frequently.

Thimble: This is optional but helpful.

Small scissors: These will be used for trimming and thread clipping.

Straight pins

Chalk marker: Choose one that dispenses from a tiny wheel.

Basting thread: Buy less-expensive white or cream-colored thread for temporary basting.

Sandpaper board: This handy tool makes marking piecing and appliqué lines easier.

Sewing machine: Make sure to use an accurate ¼" seam allowance for assembling the blocks.

Making Templates

To make a window template, lay see-through template plastic over the blade pattern on page 70 and trace it with a permanent marker. Using a ruler and rotary cutter, cut (very carefully because the plastic is slippery) the straight edges, the two outer and the two inner ones. Then use sharp scissors to cut the curves. The cut-out area in the center is your window.

This template can be used to audition fabrics before buying them. It is also used for cutting the fabric blades. What you see inside the window is what will actually appear on the blades because the seam allowances are under the plastic.

Fig. 1–2. Examples of using a window template to select blade motifs.

The patterns given for the full, half, and quarter circles are finished size. Trace these onto template plastic and cut them out. Trace the plastic templates on the right side of your fabric. The drawn line is your appliqué line. Remember to cut about ³⁄₁₆" away from the drawn line to create a turn-under allowance. The straight sides of the half and quarter circles can be cut by using a rotary cutter and ruler. Use full ¼" seam allowances on the straight sides because they will be incorporated into the seams as the blocks are assembled.

Making Plates

Cutting plate blades. Because the blades will be pieced and then appliquéd to a base block, no grain line considerations are necessary. Cutting the blades off-grain is permitted and usually highly desirable. You will be looking for the most interesting combination of motifs for each plate instead of at the grain line.

Lay your pressed fabric right side up on a table. Move your window template over the fabric, checking the area displayed in the template. Take your time doing this. You will be pleasantly surprised at what motif combinations are available (Fig. 1–2).

As you can see from the examples in Fig. 1–3, moving the template around a single main motif yields many options, all of which would be wonderful. Cut the motif you like most first. I've been known to try cutting that one last, only to find that I don't have enough fabric or that I've cut other motifs so close to my favorite one that I can no longer fit the entire template on the fabric.

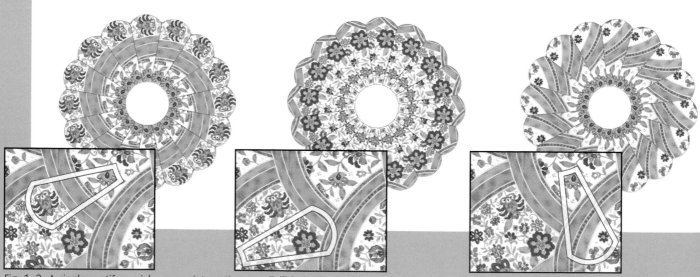

Fig. 1–3. A single motif provides many interesting possibilities.

You will have so much fun auditioning the possibilities that you may need to remind yourself to make a decision and begin cutting. Because the fabric near the selvages can be distorted as it is printed, it is better to choose your original motif near the center of the fabric. You can check the motifs near the selvages for other blades in the set, and if they match, great. If not, look elsewhere.

When you have found your favorite motif, hold the template in place and carefully trace around the outside edge. I like to use markers that I am sure can be removed, such as the white or silver pencils or soapstone markers. I do not like water- or air-soluble markers because of the chemical base.

Remove the template. With your fingers, pinch the fabric near one end of the traced blade and, using the tips of your scissors, make a small clip (Fig. 1–4). Do not cut into the fabric from the outside edge because it ruins that entire section of fabric for cutting more blades.

After making the clip, carefully cut out the blade, cutting away the drawn line. Remember, you traced around the template shape, so the actual blade size is contained within the pencil line. Using chalk or some other removable marker, make a small mark on the right side of the first blade so that you know it is the original blade. You will be using the original to cut 15 more identical ones. Here's how:

Look for the next occurrence of your chosen motif. Most designs seem to run either across the fabric or diagonally. Lay the original blade on the fabric, aligning the designs exactly. Now use the tip of your scissors to make a small cut near one end of the blade and carefully cut around the motif. Cut as close to the original blade as possible without shaving anything off the original. Shaving would make the blade smaller, and each time you use it, the original and the new blade will become progressively smaller, eventually making all the blades useless. Resist the urge to cut roughly around the blade. Rough cutting wastes fabric, and you may cut into the next set of blades.

Fig. 1–4. Clip a pinch of fabric to start your cut.

IMPORTANT: Cut the entire first set of blades before auditioning for the second. Trying to cut multiple sets of blades at one time can lead to problems because some designs overlap, making a second cut near them impossible. Take it one step at a time, and you will be fine.

Always using the original blade, continue cutting until you have a total of 16 blades for a full plate, eight for a half, and four for a quarter. Refer to your chosen pattern to determine which combination of blades is necessary for the design.

As you cut, lay the blades out in the plate shape to give you an idea of what the repeat looks like where the blades come together. You can determine within three or four blades whether you like the design or not. Nothing says you need to continue cutting if you don't like what you have. Better to stop cutting, audition another motif, and go on.

As you place the blades side by side, you will see interesting designs emerge that are not as apparent when you are looking at single pieces. In the JUNGLE quilt (page 31), the leaves make great-looking flame-like designs that come up out of the center circle on some plates. In FIESTA DE LOS CHILES (page 28), partial motifs make star-like designs around the circles, adding an even more festive air.

I try to set aside enough time to cut all the plates needed for a project at one time. Then I can put the "Swiss-cheese" fabric away and concentrate on the next steps to prepare the blades for sewing.

Keep each set of blades together and separate from the other sets. It is easy to mix blades and not realize it until much later in the process.

Trimming blades. Cutting around a fabric template without cutting the original blade can lead to slightly larger subsequent blades. Because of this, I like to trim my blades to size before marking and sewing them.

To do this, lay one blade on a rotary cutting mat. Lay the plastic window template on top, adjusting it so that your original motifs are inside the template's opening (Fig. 1–5a). To be absolutely precise, you can make another plastic template without the cutout, trace parts of the motifs from the original blade on the template, and use that to trim the remaining blades (Fig. 1–5b). Small inaccuracies at this point will show in the finished plate.

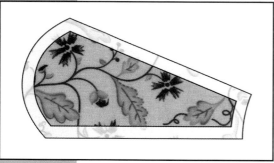

Fig. 1–5a. Window template with design centered for trimming.

Fig. 1–5b. Trimming template with fabric motiffs traced on it.

With the plastic trimming template centered on the blade, lay a ruler along the edge of the plastic and, using the rotary cutter, carefully trim the straight sides of the blade. For the top and bottom curves, it is easier to trace them and trim with scissors, or you can trace around the entire template and trim with scissors.

Because this trimming is a bit messy, I like to trim all the blades at one time and then clean up the area before marking the blades. One of the best ways to pick up all the trimmings without getting out your vacuum cleaner is to use wide sealing tape. Wind a section of it around your hand, sticky side out, and pat the cutting area. The tape picks up even the smallest bits of fiber. Now you are ready to mark your blades for piecing. The marking process is the same whether you are hand or machine piecing.

Marking blades. A sandpaper board is invaluable for marking the blades for piecing and, later, for appliqué (Fig. 1–6). The grit holds the fabric in place as you move your marking tool along the inside of the window template. If you do not have sandpaper, a piece of fabric placed beneath the blades will give you some traction. Lay the blades wrong side up on the sandpaper board. Place the window template on top of each blade, aligning the edges.

Using a marker that will be visible when you sew, mark the seam lines as shown (Fig. 1–7a). There is no need to mark the entire top of the arc because the arc will be marked on the right side of the fabric after the blades have been sewn together. All you need to mark are the corner turns so you will know where to begin stitching on the long sides (Fig. 1–7b). Mark the entire bottom arc. Keep your marker sharp and mark dark enough to see the line. Place a dot in each corner.

Mark the seam lines on each blade and stack them in a pile. I run a large basting stitch through each stack so they are easy to track. Then I take a plastic container or small bag and add a thimble, matching thread, needles, scissors, and a few pins, along with my stacks of blades. I can easily carry these with me in my purse or tote and do a bit of sewing in found moments.

Fig. 1–6. Sandpaper board.

Fig. 1–7a. Use the window template to mark the side and bottom seam lines.

Fig. 1–7b. For the arc, mark just the corner turns.

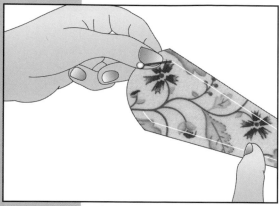

Fig. 1–8a. Pin through the dot on the top blade.

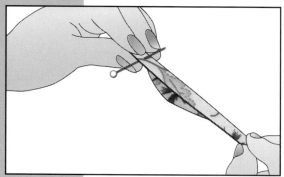

Fig. 1–8b. Pin through the dot on the bottom blade.

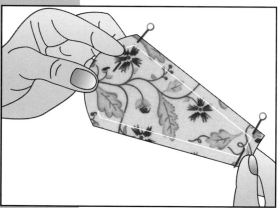

Fig. 1–9. Remove each pin and reinsert it to secure the blades.

Piecing blades. The first part of the process is the same for both hand and machine piecing. Place two blades right sides together, matching the edges. Insert a pin through the dot on the top blade and then the dot on the second blade (Fig. 1–8a). Check the second blade to be sure the pin goes through the dot (Fig. 1–8b). Do not take a bite with the pin yet. Using another pin, repeat the process with the dots at the other end of the blades.

Once these two pins have been placed, pinch the fabrics together next to the first pin. Remove the pin and reinsert it, taking a bite that bridges the seam line. Repeat this process for the second pin (Fig. 1–9). If you simply take a bite with the pins without removing them first, the second blade will shift downward slightly. The shifting will cause the motifs to be slightly out of alignment around the plate.

Now add three additional pins between the dots. As you add each pin, make sure it is coming out on the sewing line of the blade underneath. The pins should be inserted perpendicular to the fabric for correct alignment. Pinch the blades next to the pins, remove the pins, and reinsert them as described previously.

Hand piecing – The process differs for the two piecing methods. For hand piecing, I like to use all-cotton thread if possible. Choose a thread color that matches the background of your blades. A #10 needle, called a sharp, works well for me, although some people like milliner's (straw) needles. Try a variety of needles to see which is best for you. Thread your needle with approximately 18" of thread. Make a knot on the end that comes off the spool last, to help prevent tangling.

Holding the pinned blades in your left hand (if you are right-handed), pinch the blades together near the first pin at the narrow end of the blade and remove the pin. Insert the needle at the dot and take one stitch forward. Pull the thread through until the knot is at the surface of the fabric. Now make a backstitch to help reinforce this area, and begin a running stitch (Fig. 1–10 on the facing page). I usually make four or five small stitches (remember these stitches hold your plate together), check the back to be sure I have hit the line on that blade as well, pull the needle and thread through, make a backstitch, and begin again. If I make a backstitch every time I pull the needle through, I don't forget to do it, and my seams are stronger (Fig. 1–11).

Continue stitching until you reach the last pin. Remember to check that you are staying on the line on both blades. Pinch the fabrics together near the last pin, remove the pin, and bring the needle up directly at the dot. Pull the thread through and make a double backstitch, bringing the needle up through the dot for each stitch (Fig. 1–12). Cut the thread, leaving a tail about 1⁄16" long.

This is the exciting part. Pull the blades open to see how the design looks. Each time you add a blade, the design continues to take shape. This is the time when those tiny extras, like the stars on FIESTA (page 28) or the leaves on JUNGLE (page 31), become apparent.

Continue to add blades in this manner. My preference is to add the new blade to the back each time, that is, I piece blades 1 and 2, then add 3 to 2, and 4 to 3, etc. You can piece however you like, as long as you end up with a circle of 16 blades.

Machine piecing – Use a new #11 needle in your machine, 100-percent cotton thread for both needle and bobbin, and 12 stitches per inch. After pinning as described for hand piecing, begin at the wide end of the blade, inserting the needle into the dot (Fig. 1–13). Stitch forward about three stitches, backstitch just to the dot, and then stitch to the dot at the end of the blade. Stay on the drawn line and make sure to sew to the dot at the narrow end. Backstitch at the dot. Add blades as described previously until you have a total of 16.

Fig. 1–10. Start with a backstitch.

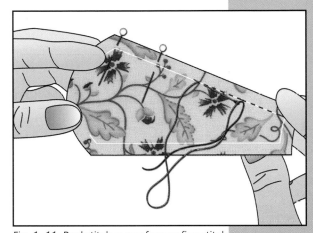
Fig. 1–11. Backstitch every four or five stitches.

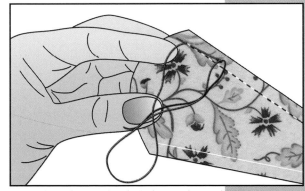
Fig. 1–12. Take two backstitches at the end of the seam line.

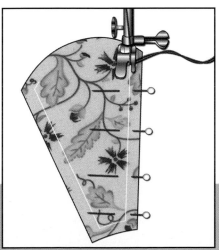
Fig. 1–13. Sew from dot to dot, beginning at the wide end of the blades.

Give it a try: For those who are contemplating hand piecing for the first time, it probably sounds like rocket science…it's not. Take it step by step and give it a try. It actually takes less time to hand piece the plates than it does to take the blades on and off the machine. Trust me…I used to do all machine piecing and have converted to doing a lot of hand piecing. It's an excellent medium for on-the-go, busy people…like you!

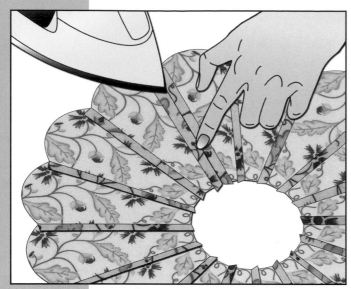

Fig. 1–14. Pressing seam allowances open.

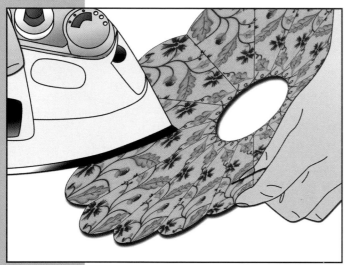

Fig. 1–15. Pressing seam allowances to one side.

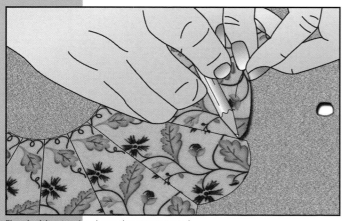

Fig. 1–16a. Mark where the seams end.

Trimming and Pressing

After the plate is pieced, trim the seam allowances to ¼". While this may only require taking off a few strays, I find that having the seam allowances more uniform makes the quilting process easier. You could choose not to do this step if it seems too tedious for you.

Set your iron to a cotton setting and use steam to press the seams as you sewed them. This step makes the seams lie flat and sets the stitches into the fabric. Now comes a decision, to press the seam allowances open or to one side. If they are pressed to one side, a dimensional element is created that I find competes with the plate designs. However, it does make the decision of where to quilt the plates easier – in the ditch. For my work, I like a flatter look, so I choose to press the seam allowances open.

To press them open, lay the plate wrong side up on the ironing surface. Use the tip of the iron and your fingers to open the first seam allowance. Press it open from the wide end to the narrow end (Fig. 1–14). Continue around the plate. Turn the plate over and press again from the right side, checking for pleats and wrinkles.

If you decide to press the seam allowances to the side, set the seam first, then lay the plate right side up on the ironing surface. Turn the seam allowance toward the blade it will lie under. Use the side of the iron to press the seam in place (Fig. 1–15). Continue around the plate in this manner.

Step back and take a look – pretty impressive, isn't it! All the cutting, trimming, piecing, and pressing combine to make irresistibly wonderful plates.

Marking for Appliqué

Place the plate back on your sandpaper board, right side up. Using a chalk marker, make a small dash where the seams end at the wide end of each blade. This junction will be easier to see if you pull back one side of the blade (Fig. 1–16a).

Align the inner edge of your plastic window template with the dashes on the plate. Align the edges evenly so that the apex of the curve will come in the same place on each blade. On each blade, trace the inside curve to use as your appliqué line (Fig. 1–16b).

Completing the Blocks

After the plates have been marked for appliquéing, cut your background blocks and baste the plates and center circles in place. If you are making full plates, cut the background fabric into 14½" squares. For other plate configurations, see the specific pattern for details.

Fold the fabric square into quarters, remembering to fold it in half one way, lightly press, reopen the fabric, refold the other way, then press again. Folding the block into a quarter square and then pressing across the two folds at the same time will not give you a true center. (Fold half plate backgrounds in half on the long sides. Fold quarter plate squares diagonally and align the center seam line of the plate with the fold.)

Lay the background fabric right side up on a flat surface. Place the plate, right side up, on top of the background, aligning the quarter marks with the seam lines on the plate. Pin in place. Using basting thread, baste about ½" in from the drawn line at the wide end of the blades. This is temporary stitching and doesn't have to be pretty (Fig. 1–17).

Also, using thread to match the plate, baste within the ¼" seam allowance at the center of the plate. This is permanent basting and should be done with care and regular sewing thread, not basting thread (Fig. 1–18).

At this point, I like to press the block from the wrong side. It allows any fullness to be worked out, and it helps keep the two layers from shifting as you appliqué.

I like to appliqué with a ⅛" to ³⁄₁₆" turn-under allowance. Usually, this means that I need to trim fabric from the top of the blades before appliquéing. Sometimes I do this a couple of blades at a time. Sometimes I

Fig. 1–16b. Trace the curve on each blade.

Fig. 1–17. Baste the outer edge of the plate to the background square.

Fig. 1–18. Baste inside the seam allowance in the center of the plate.

trim the entire plate all at once. See which works best for you. If, as you are appliquéing, the allowance forms pleats under the top of the blade, the allowance is too wide and should be trimmed.

Beginning at the dip between blades and using regular sewing thread to match the plate fabric, bring the needle up inside the fold to place the knot. Using needle-turn appliqué, turn the allowance to the back and use a blind-hem stitch along the edge. Remember to follow the drawn line. It's easy to lose the curve near the dips. Continue around the entire plate, ending with a small knot on the back of the block, under the plate.

For the center circles, I have auditioned as many as 11 fabrics to find the right one. Tempting as it may be to use multiple fabrics for the circles, I don't recommend doing that. You want the plates to take center stage, and different circle fabrics can draw the eye away from the plates.

If you need ideas for the center circle color, try using the colored dots on the selvages of your main fabric. Buy ¼-yard pieces of several colors and cut fabric circles to try. It is extremely difficult to get enough distance to judge the effectiveness of a fabric wadded into a ball and held against the plate.

A design wall is ideal for auditioning fabrics for the center circles. The wall can be as simple as a length of flannel or a flannel-backed tablecloth hung on the wall. Place the plates on the design wall and pin the circles to the plates. Step back to assess the visual impact. Sometimes you may have to cut a number of circles from the same fabric and place them on several plates to be able to judge the fabric's effectiveness. Don't

consider this wasteful. Have you ever watched artists mix paint? They mix and decide, discard, and start again.

Once you've decided on your circle fabric, lay your fabric, right side up, on the sandpaper board. Trace around the center circle template with your marking pencil, allowing ½" between tracings. The drawn line is your appliqué line. Cut out the circles with a scant ¼" (about ³⁄₁₆") allowance. Half and quarter circles are cut the same way, but you can cut the straight sides with a rotary cutter, if you like. Just place the ¼" line of the ruler on the straight lines and cut.

Center the circle over the hole in the plate. At this point, I use a ruler to measure from the dips in the plate's edge to the drawn circle to make sure I have the circle centered correctly. Be sure to measure to the inside of the drawn line because pencil lines vary in width. Pin the circle in place. Using basting thread, baste ½" inside the drawn line.

Use matching sewing thread to appliqué the circle in place. For half and quarter plates, appliqué the curve and then, without breaking the thread, baste within the ¼" allowance on the straight sides. This is permanent basting.

I do not cut away the background behind the plates. I enjoy the three-dimensional effect that the extra layer of fabric provides. To my eye, trimming away the background makes the plate recede. Press the plate from the wrong side on a padded surface.

Quilt Assembly

Make the number of full, half, and quarter blocks specified for the quilt pattern you are making. Refer to the quilt assembly diagrams for arranging the blocks and any sashing. Sew the blocks together in rows, then sew the rows together. Quilts with blocks set on point are sewn in diagonal rows. The rows are then sewn together, and the corner triangles are added last.

Piping

Cut ¾"-wide strips from the piping fabric. Piece them together, end to end, as needed. Fold the strips in half lengthwise, wrong sides together, and press. Measure through the center of the quilt in both directions to find its dimensions. Cut piping strips to those lengths. Starting with two opposite sides, align the piping strip's raw edges with the raw edges of the quilt top. Machine baste in place with a scant ¼" seam allowance. Repeat for the remaining sides, allowing the piping to overlap in the corners.

Borders

To measure for the borders, fold the quilt in half and lay it on a stable surface. This is especially important for blocks set on point where you will be measuring across the bias, which will stretch if you simply try to hold it to measure.

Measure the length of the quilt through the center. Cut two border strips this length and sew them to the sides, matching centers and ends. Press the seam allowances toward the border.

Measure the quilt through the center across the width, including the newly added side borders, and cut two strips this length. Sew them to the top and bottom of the quilt.

Directional fabric – Cut three strips selvage to selvage. Cut one of the strips in half and piece a half strip to each whole strip for the top and bottom borders. Then cut the selvages from the remaining yardage. Cut two border strips the length of the yardage for the sides of the quilt.

Nondirectional fabric – Cut border strips from selvage to selvage. Sew the strips together, end to end, as needed to create the border lengths.

Backing

Some of the wider quilts require two panels for the backing. Cut the yardage in half, selvage to selvage. Then sew the two panels together lengthwise (minus selvages).

Just for fun, you may want to incorporate a sizeable piece of the plate fabric in your backing. Then, when you show your quilt to people, you can start with the backing and say, "This is what I started with…and (flinging the quilt over) this is what I did with it!" Imagine the comments, oohs and aahs that will be forthcoming. Bask in the glory – you've earned every compliment.

Quilting Ideas

The quilting on the plates should not detract from the design. You have worked to make the plates distinctive. Take time to really study the plates to see where you might be able to quilt inconspicuously. Sometimes, you can follow an outline around a shape in the fabric or create shallow scallops to fit between motifs.

On JUNGLE (page 31), BUGS (page 22), and SYMPHONY (page 25), I discovered that a shallow curve from the bottom-left corner to the center top of each blade secured the plate without overwhelming it. (See Resources, page 78, for a good tool for marking curves.)

If you have pressed your blade seam allowances to the side rather than open, quilting in the ditch between blades is an option. With allowances pressed open, however, quilting in the ditch would actually weaken the stitching. Whatever you decide, be sure the plates take center stage, not the quilting.

To develop a quilting design, I sometimes place a piece of tracing paper over a line drawing of my quilt top. Then I just doodle designs until I like what I see. I have been known to quilt for several hours only to find that what I thought would be fabulous is not. I then had to rip it out and try again. The tracing idea has all but eliminated the ripping.

Behind the plates, I've used straight-line grids, meandering lines, and radiating lines. For the quilts presented in this book, I tried to do something a bit different on each of them. Not only was it more visually appealing, it was more fun to do as well.

My hope is that you will enjoy making Dresden Plates and that you will come to know the joy and contentment that the cutting, hand piecing, and hand appliqué can bring to your life. Quiltmaking has enriched my life in so many ways. May it do the same for you.

CHAPTER TWO

Quilt Patterns

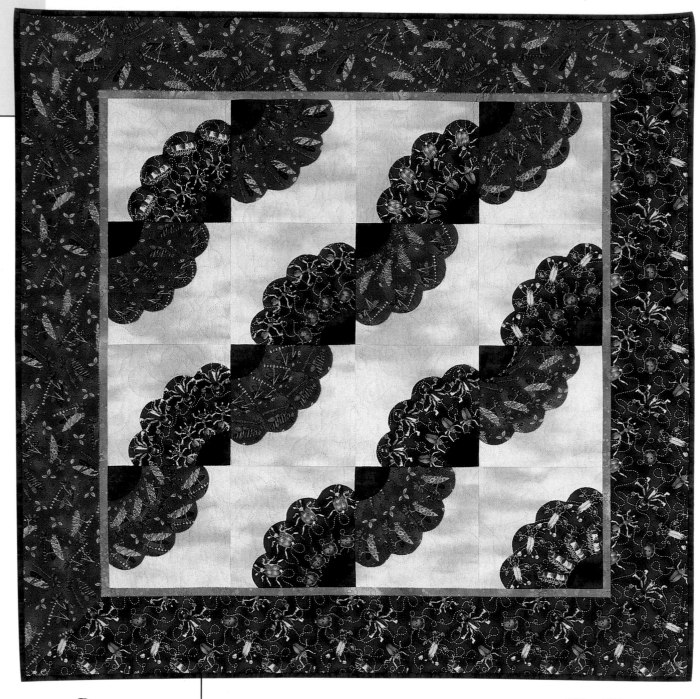

BUGS

39" x 39"

Bugs

Yardage

Plates:
4 repeats of 8 motifs from each of two fabrics, plus ⅜ yard of each fabric for a two-color outer border.

Other Fabrics	Yards
Quarter circles	⅛
Background	1
Inner border	¼
Backing	1¼
Binding	½
Batting	43" x 43"

Cutting

Outer border:
Cut (2) 5½" strips, selvage to selvage, from each plate fabric, before cutting plates.

Plates:
Cut blades for 16 quarter plates.

Circles:
Cut 16 quarter circles.

Background:
Cut (16) 7½" squares.

Inner border:
Cut (4) 1" strips, selvage to selvage.

Binding:
Cut (5) 2¼" strips, selvage to selvage.

Anyone would welcome these critters into her home. With bright smiling faces and snazzy shoes, these charmers will enliven any wall. Whimsical novelty fabrics like these make delightful Dresden Plates.

Originally, I bought enough of both fabrics to make a quilt from each. When I started cutting the blades, there were not enough different repeats to be interesting, but combined, the fabrics were fabulous.

Because I wanted to use the main fabrics as a border, I added a narrow accent border. Otherwise, the plates would have "bled" into the outer border, reducing their effectiveness.

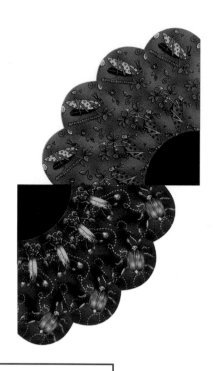

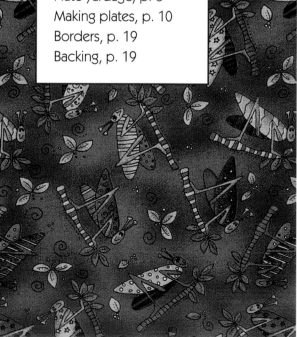

Quilt assembly

Follow the quilt assembly diagram to arrange and sew the blocks, butted inner borders, and mitered outer borders.

Quilting ideas

Gentle curves add movement to the blades. There are seven dragonflies quilted amid the meandering designs in the background. The narrow border is quilted in the ditch, and a cable design completes the larger border. The quilting thread was changed to match each border and blade fabric.

Finishing

Layer the quilt top, batting, and backing. Baste and quilt the layers. Trim the extra batting and backing even with the quilt top. Use a continuous binding strip, folded in half lengthwise right side out, to bind the raw edges.

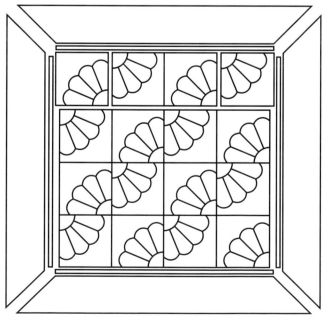

Quilt assembly.

53½" x 73½"

SYMPHONY

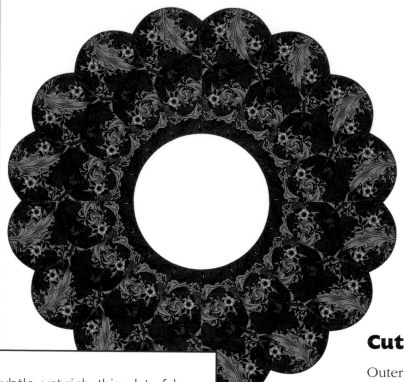

Yardage

Plates: 16 repeats of 12 motifs.

Other Fabrics	Yards
Circles	⅜
Background	3¼
Inner border	⅜
Outer border	
directional fabric,	2½
or nondirectional	2
Backing	4⅝
Binding	⅝
Batting	60" x 80"

Cutting

Outer border:
Cut (4) 6½" strips the length of the fabric.
See page 19 for cutting directional fabrics.

Plates: Cut blades for 8 full, 6 half, and 4 quarter plates.

Circles: Cut 8 full, 6 half, and 4 quarter circles.

Background:
- Cut (8) 14½" squares.
- Cut (2) 21⅛" squares. Cut the squares twice diagonally for the side triangles (half plates). There will be two extra triangles.
- Cut (2) 10⅞" squares. Cut the squares once diagonally for the corner triangles (quarter plates).

Inner border:
Cut (6) 1½" strips, selvage to selvage.

Backing: Cut the yardage in half crosswise to make 2 panels.

Binding:
Cut (7) 2¼" strips selvage to selvage.

Subtle, yet rich, this plate fabric was a joy to work with. The background fabric is from the same collection, with a complementary pattern that enhances the plates. A narrow green inner border separates the plates from the outer border of the same fabric.

This quilt contains the equivalent of 12 plates: eight full ones, three plates divided into halves, and one plate quartered for the corners.

Quilt assembly

Follow the quilt assembly diagram to arrange and sew the blocks and butted borders.

Quilting ideas

The blades are quilted with a shallow curve, and the centers have a curved triangular shape that was taken from the background quilting. The narrow border is outlined in the ditch, then it has a row of tiny scallops that point toward the center. An interlocking cable design enhances the outer border.

Finishing

Layer the quilt top, batting, and backing. Baste and quilt the layers. Trim the extra batting and backing even with the quilt top. Use a continuous binding strip, folded in half lengthwise right side out, to bind the raw edges.

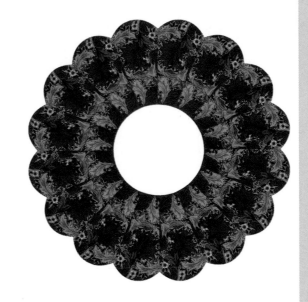

Quilt assembly.

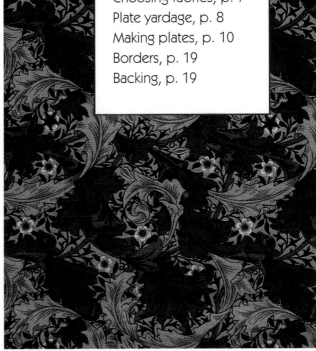

Find it Fast

Patterns
Blade, p. 70
Circles, pgs. 70 and 71

Techniques
Choosing fabrics, p. 7
Plate yardage, p. 8
Making plates, p. 10
Borders, p. 19
Backing, p. 19

FIESTA DE LOS CHILES

54½" x 54½"

FIESTA DE LOS CHILES

Yardage

Plates: 16 repeats of 8 motifs.

Other Fabrics	Yards
Circles	¼
Background	2 ½
Inner border	½
Outer border	
directional fabric,	2
or nondirectional	1 ¾
Backing	3 ½
Binding	½
Batting	61" x 61"

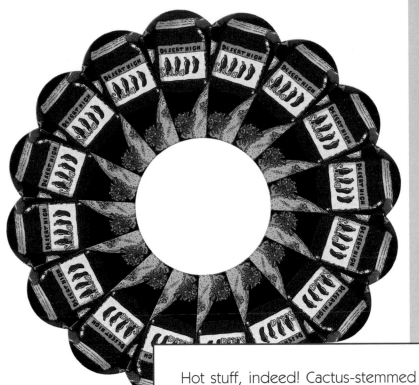

Cutting

Plates: Cut blades for 5 full, 4 half, and 4 quarter plates.

Circles: Cut 5 full, 4 half, and 4 quarter circles.

Background:
- Cut (5) 14½" squares.
- Cut (1) 21⅛" squares. Cut the square twice diagonally for the side triangles (half plates).
- Cut (2) 10⅞" squares. Cut the squares once diagonally for the corner triangles (quarter plates).

Inner border:
Cut (5) 2" strips, selvage to selvage.

Outer border:
Cut (4) 6½" strips the length of the fabric. See page 19 for cutting directional fabrics.

Backing: Cut the yardage in half crosswise to make 2 panels.

Binding:
Cut (6) 2¼" strips, selvage to selvage.

Hot stuff, indeed! Cactus-stemmed margarita glasses, tequila and margarita bottles, and chile peppers, all on a lime green background. I must admit that the green fabric was not my favorite color when I bought it, but it is perfect for showcasing these plates. As I quilted the piece, I found myself liking the entire effect more and more, and now this quilt is one of my favorites.

Notice the star points formed around the circle on the margarita glasses…one of those serendipitous effects. The narrow blue border gives a nice break between the activity in the center of the quilt and the main-fabric outer border.

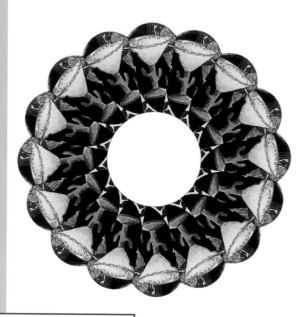

Quilt assembly

Follow the quilt assembly diagram to arrange and sew the blocks and butted borders.

Quilting ideas

The plates are carefully quilted along fabric pattern lines to anchor them without detracting from them. For instance, the margarita glasses are quilted along the V-shaped bowl, and the bottles along the label lines. The background is meander quilted, and the inner and outer borders contain different sizes of cable designs.

Finishing

Layer the quilt top, batting, and backing. Baste and quilt the layers. Trim the extra batting and backing even with the quilt top. Use a continuous binding strip, folded in half lengthwise right side out, to bind the raw edges.

Find it Fast

Patterns
Blade, p. 70
Circles, pgs. 70 and 71

Techniques
Choosing fabrics, p. 7
Plate yardage, p. 8
Making plates, p. 10
Borders, p. 19
Backing, p. 19

Quilt assembly.

45" x 61"

Dresden Plates of Distinction   *Sharon Stroud*

The giraffes "spoke" to me! I could see them, proud and strong, with their necks touching around a center circle. The rest of the animals and birds came along for the ride. Notice the leopard's head? What is really a tree trunk became a party hat. That's the fun of this technique…surprises are always cropping up.

When cutting the borders, I was not paying attention to which animals fell within each border strip. The giraffe spoke again, very loudly! Partial giraffe bodies drew the eye away from the center plates, so I cut again, centering the giraffes within each border strip. As you may guess, selectively cutting these borders took almost as much fabric as the plates themselves, but to great effect.

Yardage

Plates: 16 repeats of 6 motifs.

Other Fabrics	Yards
Circles	⅛
Background	1½
Sashing	¾
Cornerstones	⅛
Border	
directional fabric,	2⅛
or nondirectional	1¼
Backing	4
Binding	½
Batting	51" x 67"

Cutting

Plates: Cut blades for 6 full plates.

Circles: Cut 6 full circles.

Background: Cut (6) 14½" squares.

Sashing: Cut (17) 2½" x 14½" rectangles.

Cornerstones: Cut (12) 2½" squares.

Border:
Cut (6) 6" strips the width of the fabric. See page 19 for cutting directional fabrics.

Backing: Cut yardage in half, selvage to selvage to make two panels.

Binding: Cut (6) 2¼" strips, selvage to selvage.

Quilt assembly

Follow the quilt assembly diagram to arrange and sew the blocks, sashing, and butted border.

Quilting ideas

The blades have been quilted with a shallow curve, and the center circles have a double-leaf design. The background has been quilted with radiating lines to highlight the plates, while the sashing has a rope-like cable. The cornerstones are outlined ⅜" in from the seams. The outer border contains fan quilting.

Finishing

Layer the quilt top, batting, and backing. Baste and quilt the layers. Trim the extra batting and backing even with the quilt top. Use a continuous binding strip, folded in half lengthwise right side out, to bind the raw edges.

Quilt assembly.

Find it Fast

Patterns
Blade, p. 70
Circles, pgs. 70 and 71

Techniques
Choosing fabrics, p. 7
Plate yardage, p. 8
Making plates, p. 10
Borders, p. 19
Backing, p. 19

FINE CHINA

42" x 42"

FINE CHINA

Yardage

Plates: 16 repeats of 4 motifs.

Other Fabrics	Yards
Circles	⅛
Background	1
Sashing	½
Border	⅝
Backing	2⅝
Binding	½
Batting	46" x 46"

Cutting

Plates:
Cut blades for 4 full plates.

Circles:
Cut 4 full circles.

Background:
Cut (4) 14½" squares.

Cornerstones:
Cut (9) 2½" squares

Sashing:
Cut (12) 2½" x 14½" rectangles.

Border:
Cut (4) 4½" strips selvage to selvage.

Backing:
Cut the yardage in half crosswise to make 2 panels.

Binding:
Cut (5) 2¼" strips, selvage to selvage.

This is the quilt that started it all. With only one yard of fabric and an idea, I began cutting blades. You will notice that three of the plates are predominantly rose, and the other is mostly blue, the result of having too little fabric and being forced to settle for the fabric left after cutting my best choices. Having learned that lesson early, I now buy at least one-half yard more than I think I will need.

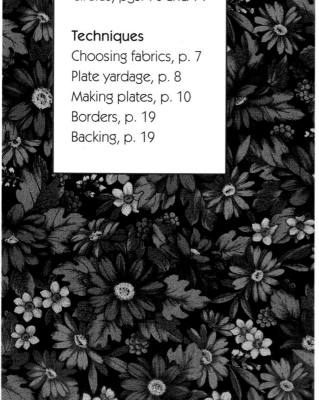

Find it Fast
Patterns
Blade, p. 70
Circles, pgs. 70 and 71

Techniques
Choosing fabrics, p. 7
Plate yardage, p. 8
Making plates, p. 10
Borders, p. 19
Backing, p. 19

Quilt assembly

Follow the quilt assembly diagram to arrange and sew the blocks, sashing, and butted border.

Quilting ideas

This piece is heavily quilted. The plates are outlined, and the background is crosshatched. The sashing is quilted ⅜" in from the edges, with a single cable within that quilting. The cornerstones are quilted ⅜" in from the edges, and a fan design enhances the blue border.

Finishing

Layer the quilt top, batting, and backing. Baste and quilt the layers. Trim the extra batting and backing even with the quilt top. Use a continuous binding strip, folded in half lengthwise right side out, to bind the raw edges.

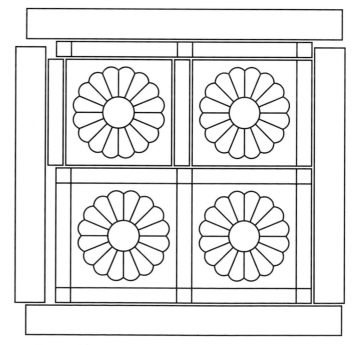

Quilt assembly.

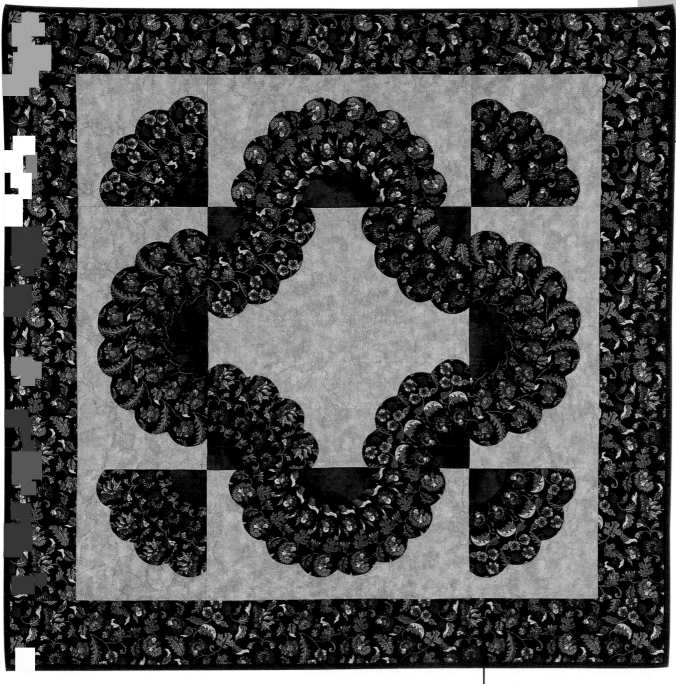

35" x 35"

JACOBEAN GARDEN

JACOBEAN GARDEN

Yardage

Plates:
16 repeats of 2 motifs and 8 repeats of 4 different motifs.

Other Fabrics	Yards
Circles	⅛
Background	1⅛
Border	⅝
Backing	1¼
Binding	⅜
Batting	39" x 39"

Cutting

Plates:
Cut blades for 2 full and 8 quarter plates.

Circles:
Cut 4 half and 8 quarter circles.

Background:
- Cut (1) 14½" square
- Cut (4) 7½" squares
- Cut (4) 7½" x 14½" rectangles

Border:
Cut (4) 4" strips, selvage to selvage.

Binding:
Cut (4) 2¼" strips, selvage to selvage.

The flowers on this fabric seemed made for the blade template. The half plates are done in pairs set opposite each other. The quarter plates are cut in pairs, with one quarter plate inside the center square and the other in the corner. The flower colors are vibrant against the black background.

Quilt assembly

Follow the quilt assembly diagram to arrange and sew the blocks and butted border.

Quilting ideas

While the plates themselves are quilted with a simple curved design, the center contains a design reminiscent of the fabric print, with straight lines radiating from behind it. All the plates were outlined, and the outer background was quilted with a stipple pattern which forms irregular hearts. The border is quilted with a cable design.

Finishing

Layer the quilt top, batting, and backing. Baste and quilt the layers. Trim the extra batting and backing even with the quilt top. Use a continuous binding strip, folded in half lengthwise right side out, to bind the raw edges.

Find it Fast

Patterns
Blade, p. 70
Circles, pgs. 70 and 71

Techniques
Choosing fabrics, p. 7
Plate yardage, p. 8
Making plates, p. 10
Borders, p. 19
Backing, p. 19

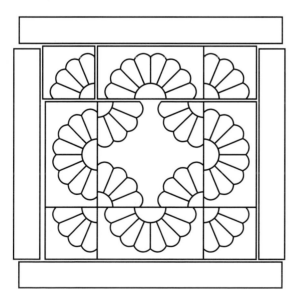

Quilt assembly.

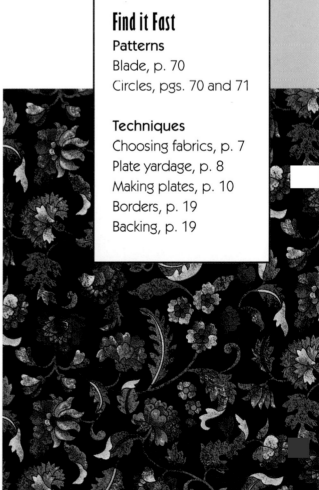

NIGHT BLOOMS

38" x 38"

NIGHT BLOOMS

Yardage

Plates:
16 repeats of two motifs and 8 repeats of 4 different motifs.

Other Fabrics	Yards
Circles	⅛
Background	1⅛
Piping	⅛
Outer border	¾
Backing	1¼
Binding	⅜
Batting	42" x 42"

Cutting

Plates:
Cut blades for 1 full and 12 quarter plates.

Circles:
Cut 1 full and 12 quarter circles.

Background:
- Cut (1) 14½" square.
- Cut (4) 7½" squares.
- Cut (4) 7½" x 14½" rectangles.

Border:
Cut (4) 5½" strips, selvage to selvage.

Binding:
Cut (4) 2¼" strips, selvage to selvage.

The plate fabric was wonderful to work with because it presented many design possibilities. The daisy-like flower was especially bright and eye-catching, so I used it in every plate. The center plate has a lot of the daisy motif, while the quarter plates have it in smaller amounts. With the daisies spread throughout the quilt top in varying amounts, the eye moves readily over the entire surface. Notice also the four rounds of motifs in the center plate: tulips, large daisy, small daisy, and small blue flowers.

So that the plate fabric could be used for the border, I chose to add an accent of ⅛" finished flat piping to separate the corner plates from the border fabric. Though small, the piping does the job beautifully.

Find it Fast

Patterns

Blade, p. 70
Circles, pgs. 70 and 71

Techniques

Choosing fabrics, p. 7
Plate yardage, p. 8
Making plates, p. 10
Borders, p. 19
Backing, p. 19

Quilt assembly

Follow the quilt assembly diagram to arrange and sew the blocks, piping, and butted border.

Quilting ideas

The plates and circles were outline quilted, then the blades were quilted in scallops and curves. The background is quilted in straight intersecting lines to give the illusion of garden paths, while the border has a continuous heart design.

Finishing

Layer the quilt top, batting, and backing. Baste and quilt the layers. Trim the extra batting and backing even with the quilt top. Use a continuous binding strip, folded in half lengthwise right side out, to bind the raw edges.

Quilt assembly.

37" x 37"

GOODNIGHT MOON

Yardage

Plates:
8 repeats of 4 motifs from each of 2 fabrics.

Other Fabrics	Yards
Quarter circles	⅛
Background	1
Border	¾
Backing	1⅛
Binding	⅜
Batting	41" x 41"

Cutting

Plates:
Cut blades for 16 quarter-plates.

Circles:
Cut 16 quarter-circles.

Background:
Cut (16) 7½" squares.

Border:
Cut (4) 5" strips, selvage to selvage.

Binding:
Cut (4) 2¼" strips, selvage to selvage.

The use of two colorways of the same fabric makes this quilt more interesting, while the paler colors make it restful. Because only the purple blocks touch the border, I was able to use the blue moon fabric for the border, without adding piping or an accent color.

If you look closely at the photo, you will notice that there are four different pairs of blue quarter plates and one pair of purple quarter plates in the center. The other six quarter plates are purple, and each one is different.

Quilt assembly

Follow the quilt assembly diagram to arrange and sew the blocks and butted border.

Quilting ideas

The plates are quilted with wavy lines and scallops, while the background has an interlocking pattern that creates a sense of motion. The border is quilted with a large egg-and-dart motif, with stars in the egg portion.

Finishing

Layer the quilt top, batting, and backing. Baste and quilt the layers. Trim the extra batting and backing even with the quilt top. Use a continuous binding strip, folded in half lengthwise right side out, to bind the raw edges.

Find it Fast

Patterns
Blade, p. 70
Circles, pgs. 70 and 71

Techniques
Choosing fabrics, p. 7
Plate yardage, p. 8
Making plates, p. 10
Borders, p. 19
Backing, p. 19

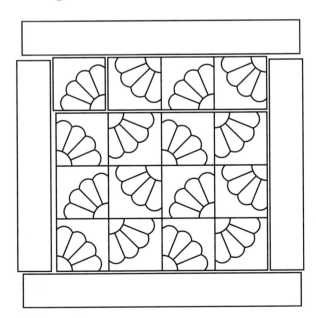

Quilt assembly.

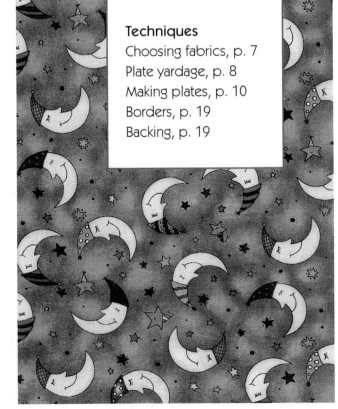

PINE CONES

37" x 37"

PINE CONES

Yardage

Plates: 16 repeats of 4 motifs.

Other Fabrics	Yards
Circles	⅛
Background	1
Border	¾
Backing	1¼
Binding	⅜
Batting	41" x 41"

Cutting

Plates:
Cut blades for 1 full, 4 half, and 4 quarter plates.

Circles:
Cut 1 full, 4 half, and 4 quarter circles.

Background:
- Cut (1) 14½" square.
- Cut (4) 7½" squares.
- Cut (4) 7½" x 14½" rectangles.

Border:
Cut (4) 5" strips, selvage to selvage.

Binding:
Cut (4) 2¼" strips, selvage to selvage.

The look and feel of this quilt is quietly elegant. The pine cone fabric is one that I could have played with indefinitely – there were so many possibilities. The quilt contains the equivalent of four full plates, with one left whole, two divided into four half plates, and one quartered for the four corners.

Find it Fast

Patterns
Blade, p. 70
Circles, pgs. 70 and 71

Techniques
Choosing fabrics, p. 7
Plate yardage, p. 8
Making plates, p. 10
Borders, p. 19
Backing, p. 19

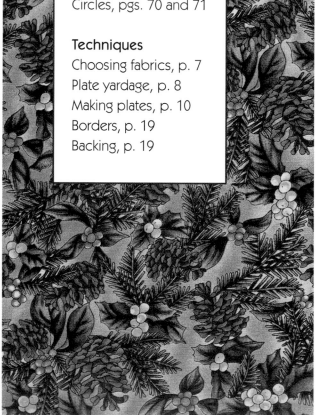

Quilt assembly

Follow the quilt assembly diagram to arrange and sew the blocks and butted border.

Quilting ideas

I know you will find this hard to believe (I did, even as I was doing it!), but the blades are quilted along the pine needle clusters. It was the only way to quilt the blades without detracting from the design. I also quilted in the ditch around the outside of each plate and circle. The background fabric's design lent itself to quilting center veins in each motif, rather than doing an all-over design. The border is quilted with a holly leaf and berry pattern.

Finishing

Layer the quilt top, batting, and backing. Baste and quilt the layers. Trim the extra batting and backing even with the quilt top. Use a continuous binding strip, folded in half lengthwise right side out, to bind the raw edges.

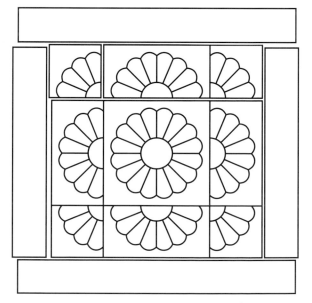

Quilt assembly.

34" x 34"

COOL CATS

Yardage

Plates: 16 repeats of 4 motifs.

Other Fabrics	Yards
Circles	⅛
Background	1
Border	½
Backing	1⅛
Binding	⅜
Batting	38" x 38"

Cutting

Plates:
Cut blades for one full plate and 12 quarter plates.

Circles:
Cut one full and 12 quarter circles.

Background:
- Cut (1) 14½" square.
- Cut (12) 7½" squares.

Border:
Cut (4) 3½" strips, selvage to selvage.

Binding:
Cut (4) 2¼" strips, selvage to selvage.

Cool cats really describes this quilt, especially the cats with the "shades." With careful cutting, I was able to use two cat faces per blade. The motifs used for the center plate were the most prominent, so I left that plate whole as a focal point. The fuchsia background was the perfect foil for the multi-colored cats, and the dark purple used for the centers and border gives the eye a resting place. This was one quilt in which the plate fabric did not work as the border – much too busy!

Quilt assembly

Follow the quilt assembly diagram to arrange and sew the blocks and butted border.

Quilting ideas

All plates and circles were outline quilted, with the central plate also quilted within the blades. I decided not to quilt within the blades on the quarter plates because I felt it would detract from the design. The background has an open basketweave pattern, and the border has an overlapping cable.

Finishing

Layer the quilt top, batting, and backing. Baste and quilt the layers. Trim the extra batting and backing even with the quilt top. Use a continuous binding strip, folded in half lengthwise right side out, to bind the raw edges.

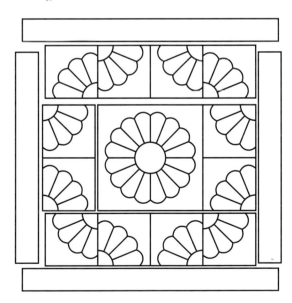

Quilt assembly.

Find it Fast

Patterns
Blade, p. 70
Circles, pgs. 70 and 71

Techniques
Choosing fabrics, p. 7
Plate yardage, p. 8
Making plates, p. 10
Borders, p. 19
Backing, p. 19

GRANDMA BASL
LOVED DANDELIONS

22" x 22"

GRANDMA BASL LOVED DANDELIONS

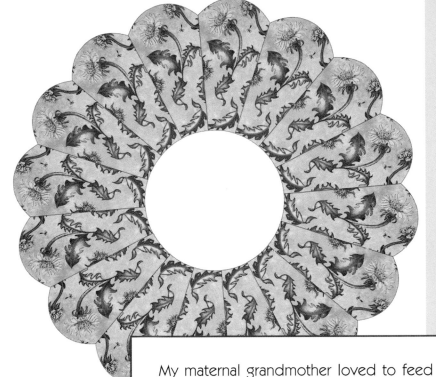

Yardage

Plate:
16 repeats of 1 motif.

Other Fabrics	Yards
Circle	⅛
Background	½
Piping	⅛
Border	⅜
Backing	¾
Binding	¼
Batting	26" x 26"

Cutting

Plate:
Cut blades for 1 full plate.

Circle:
Cut 1 full circle.

Background:
Cut (1) 14½" square.

Piping:
Cut (2) ¾" strips, selvage to selvage.

Border:
Cut (2) 4½" strips, selvage to selvage.

Binding:
Cut (3) 2¼" strips, selvage to selvage.

My maternal grandmother loved to feed her canary the first dandelions of the season, so using this fabric seemed like an ideal way to honor my grandmother. Because the dandelion motifs were similar, all the plates made from this fabric would have looked very much alike. Therefore, I chose to make only one plate and auditioned the fabric until I found the best motif. Notice the small dandelions near the edge of the blades, as well as the small leaf tips around the circle.

To bring a bit more yellow to the edge of the quilt, I added a ⅛" finished flat piping before attaching the binding.

I smile and think of my grandmother every time I see this quilt – I know she'd love it!

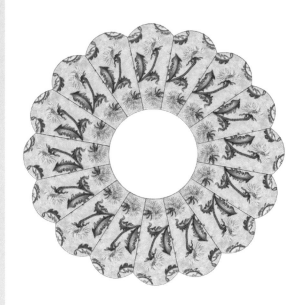

Find it Fast

Patterns
Blade, p. 70
Circles, pgs. 70 and 71

Techniques
Choosing fabrics, p. 7
Plate yardage, p. 8
Making plates, p. 10
Borders, p. 19
Backing, p. 19

Quilt assembly

Follow the quilt assembly diagram to arrange and sew the block, butted border, and piping.

Quilting ideas

There is a lot of quilting in this small piece. First, I outlined the circle and the plate to give them definition, which I always do on my quilts. The background quilting was inspired by a huge cobweb in a spruce tree that I saw while mowing the lawn. The borders are done in Baptist fans to imitate the wind blowing the seeds about.

Finishing

Layer the quilt top, batting, and backing. Baste and quilt the layers. Trim the extra batting and backing even with the quilt top. Add the piping if desired. Use a continuous binding strip, folded in half lengthwise right side out, to bind the raw edges.

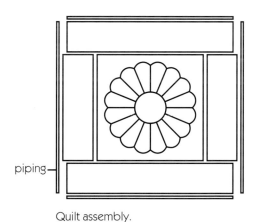

piping

Quilt assembly.

37" x 37"

HALLOWEEN FROGS

Yardage

Plates: 16 repeats of 4 motifs.

Other Fabrics	Yards
Circles	¼
Background	1
Border	¾
Backing	1¼
Binding	⅜
Batting	41" x 41"

Cutting

Plates:
Cut blades for 1 full, 4 half, and 4 quarter plates.

Circles:
Cut 1 full, 4 half, and 4 quarter circles.

Background:
- Cut (1) 14½" square.
- Cut (4) 7½" squares.
- Cut (4) 7½" x 14½" rectangles.

Border:
Cut (4) 5" strips, selvage to selvage.

Binding:
Cut (4) 2¼" strips, selvage to selvage.

Though I'm not a big fan of Halloween, I felt compelled to make a Halloween quilt with this whimsical frog fabric. I love the hats and bow ties! The leaves made great secondary designs, while the twining vines and spiders made interesting corner plates.

Quilt assembly

Follow the quilt assembly diagram to arrange and sew the blocks and butted border.

Quilting ideas

I couldn't wait to quilt this top – it begged for spider-webs behind the plates. I also quilted veins on the leaves of the half and full plates and the vine on the quarter plates. The border has a winding vine and leaf pattern that echoes the plate fabric.

Finishing

Layer the quilt top, batting, and backing. Baste and quilt the layers. Trim the extra batting and backing even with the quilt top. Use a continuous binding strip, folded in half lengthwise right side out, to bind the raw edges.

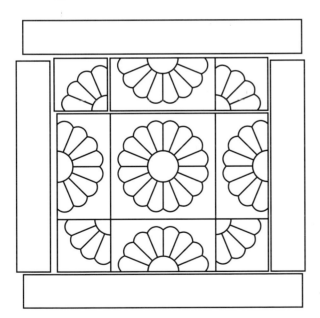

Quilt assembly.

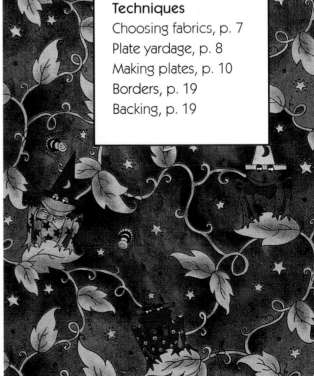

Find it Fast
Patterns
Blade, p. 70
Circles, pgs. 70 and 71

Techniques
Choosing fabrics, p. 7
Plate yardage, p. 8
Making plates, p. 10
Borders, p. 19
Backing, p. 19

POPPIES

23½" x 23½"

POPPIES

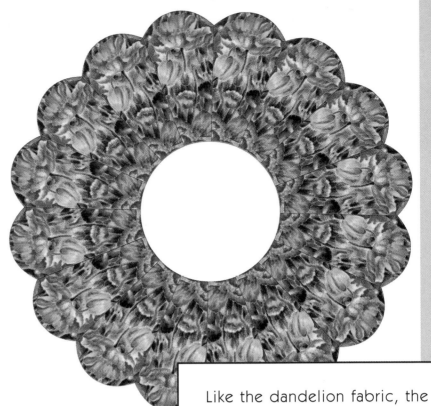

Yardage

Plates: 16 repeats of 2 motifs.

Other Fabrics	Yards
Circles	⅛
Background	⅝
Piping	⅛
Border	⅜
Backing	⅞
Binding	¼
Batting	28" x 28"

Cutting

Plates:
Cut blades for 1 full and 4 quarter plates.

Circles:
Cut 1 full and 4 quarter circles.

Background:
Cut (1) 18½" square.

Piping:
Cut (4) ¾" strips, selvage to selvage.

Border:
Cut (2) 3¼" strips, selvage to selvage.

Binding:
Cut (3) 2¼" strips, selvage to selvage.

Like the dandelion fabric, the poppies looked very similar when cut into blades. I used the equivalent of two full plates with one left intact and the other divided into quarter plates. Notice the four distinct rings in the full plate.

Because I also wanted to use the poppy fabric as a border, I sewed a ⅛" flat finished yellow piping between the blocks and the borders. The yellow piping highlights the yellow in the poppy fabric. The background fabric adds an airy feel to the quilt. All the plates are appliquéd to an 18-inch background square.

Quilt assembly

Follow the quilt assembly diagram to arrange and sew the blocks, piping, and butted border.

Quilting ideas

The circles and outside edges of the blades are quilted in the ditch. The full plate has a double row of shallow scallops to secure the blades, while the quarter plates have curved diagonal lines. The background is meander quilted, and the border has a modified cable with an oval center motif.

Finishing

Layer the quilt top, batting, and backing. Baste and quilt the layers. Trim the extra batting and backing even with the quilt top. Use a continuous binding strip, folded in half lengthwise right side out, to bind the raw edges.

Quilt assembly.

22" x 22"

HOT CHILE PEPPERS

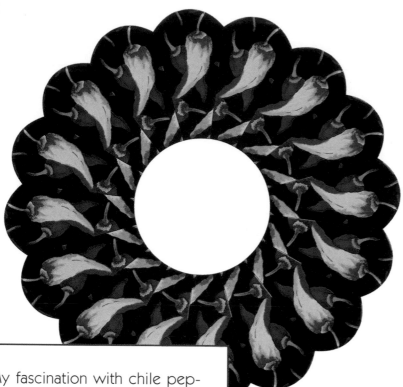

Yardage

Plates:
16 repeats of 1 motif and 4 each of 4 additional motifs.

Other Fabrics	Yards
Circles	⅛
Background	⅝
Border	⅜
Backing	¾
Binding	¼
Batting	26" x 26"

Cutting

Plates:
Cut blades for 1 full and 4 quarter plates.

Circles:
Cut 1 full and 4 quarter circles.

Background:
Cut (1) 18½" square.

Border:
Cut (3) 2½" strips, selvage to selvage.

Binding:
Cut (3) 2¼" strips, selvage to selvage.

My fascination with chile pepper fabrics continues in this quilt. Because the chiles were quite distinctive, I used one motif for the center full plate and four different motifs for the corner quarter plates.

A narrow border of the chile fabric frames the quilt perfectly because the randomness of the fabric provides an excellent counterpoint to the more controlled plates. The background fabric adds additional fire, definitely not a sedate quilt! All the plates are appliquéd to an 18-inch background square.

Quilt assembly

Follow the quilt assembly diagram to arrange and sew the block and butted border.

Quilting ideas

The plates have minimal quilting, with meander quilting in the background and a single cable in the border.

Finishing

Layer the quilt top, batting, and backing. Baste and quilt the layers. Trim the extra batting and backing even with the quilt top. Use a continuous binding strip, folded in half lengthwise right side out, to bind the raw edges.

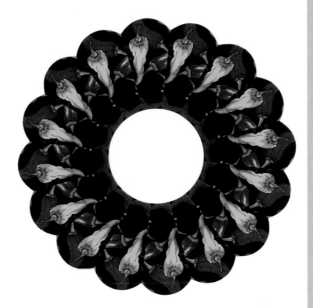

Quilt assembly.

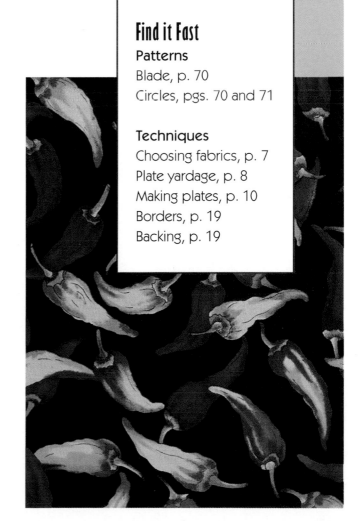

Find it Fast

Patterns
Blade, p. 70
Circles, pgs. 70 and 71

Techniques
Choosing fabrics, p. 7
Plate yardage, p. 8
Making plates, p. 10
Borders, p. 19
Backing, p. 19

DALMATIANS

21" x 21"

DALMATIANS

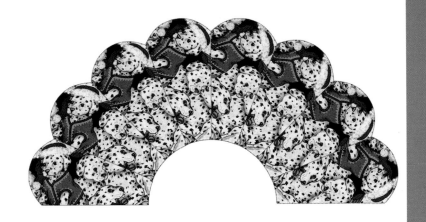

Yardage

Plates:
8 repeats of 4 motifs, plus ¼ yard for the center square.

Other Fabrics	Yards
Circles	⅛
Background	½
Backing	¾
Binding	¼
Batting	25" x 25"

Cutting

Center square:
Cut (1) 7½" square from the plate fabric before cutting plates.

Plates:
Cut blades for 4 half plates.

Circles:
Cut 4 half circles.

Background:
Cut (4) 7½" x 14½" rectangles.

Binding:
Cut (3) 2¼" strips, selvage to selvage.

DALMATIANS contains a wonderful Christmas print. The dogs' faces and attire made me laugh when I saw them. Careful thought went into the cutting of these half plates; this was not random placement. I wanted the dogs to be upright within each blade. This necessitated planning exactly which motifs would be in each half plate. If your fabric is not so directional, random placement works great. After auditioning many fabrics for the center block, I found that the Dalmatian fabric looked best.

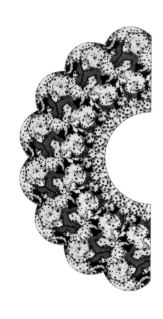

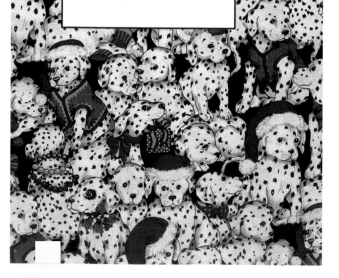

Find it Fast

Patterns

Blade, p. 70

Circles, pgs. 70 and 71

Techniques

Choosing fabrics, p. 7

Plate yardage, p. 8

Making plates, p. 10

Borders, p. 19

Backing, p. 19

Quilt assembly

Follow the quilt assembly diagram to arrange and sew the blocks and center square.

Quilting ideas

To add to the spinning effect of the half plates, I quilted curved lines radiating from the blades and a spiraling design in the center block.

Finishing

Layer the quilt top, batting, and backing. Baste and quilt the layers. Trim the extra batting and backing even with the quilt top. Use a continuous binding strip, folded in half lengthwise right side out, to bind the raw edges.

Quilt assembly.

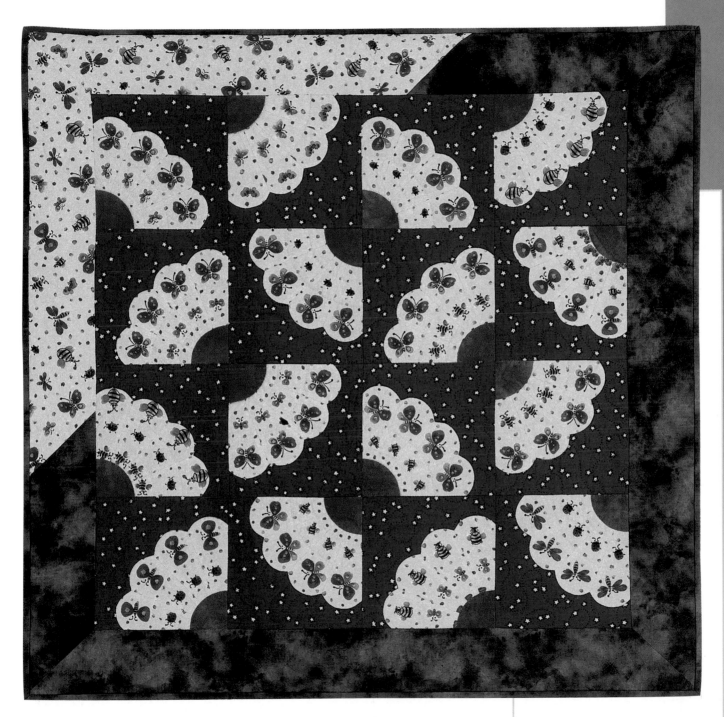

35" x 35"

YELLOW FLYERS

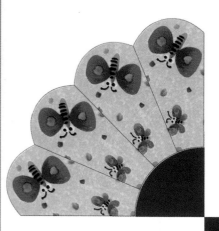

Yardage

Plates:
8 repeats of 4 motifs, plus 4 repeats of 8 different motifs. For two-color borders, buy ⅜ to ½ yard extra.

Other Fabrics	Yards
Circles	⅛
Background	1
Border	⅝
Backing	1¼
Binding	⅜
Batting	39" x 39"

Cutting

Plates:
Cut blades for 16 quarter plates.

Circles:
Cut 16 quarter circles.

Background:
Cut (16) 7½" squares.

Border:
Cut (4) 4" strips, selvage to selvage.

Binding:
Cut (4) 2¼" strips, selvage to selvage.

The motifs in this fabric were quite widely spaced, but I was able to get two distinct rounds in each blade. Each butterfly (flyer) is distinct and isolated. This quilt has four pairs of matching blades and eight different quarter plates that complete the square.

The flyer fabric in the corner border was all that remained of my plate yardage. Combining that with a contrasting fabric produced an interesting border treatment with mitered corners.

Quilt assembly

Follow the quilt assembly diagram to arrange and sew the blocks and mitered border. To make two-color border strips, piece together 4" strips with a diagonal seam.

Quilting ideas

I quilted in the ditch on some plates, quilted quarter circles between the blade motifs, meandered behind the plates, and did an egg-and-dart border.

Finishing

Layer the quilt top, batting, and backing. Baste and quilt the layers. Trim the extra batting and backing even with the quilt top. Use a continuous binding strip, folded in half lengthwise right side out, to bind the raw edges.

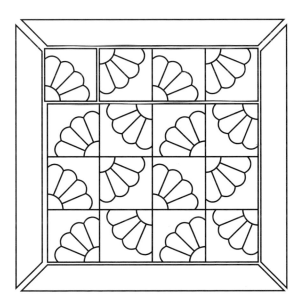

Quilt assembly.

Find it Fast

Patterns
Blade, p. 70
Circles, pgs. 70 and 71

Techniques
Choosing fabrics, p. 7
Plate yardage, p. 8
Making plates, p. 10
Borders, p. 19
Backing, p. 19

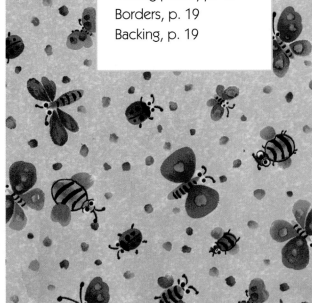

Template Patterns

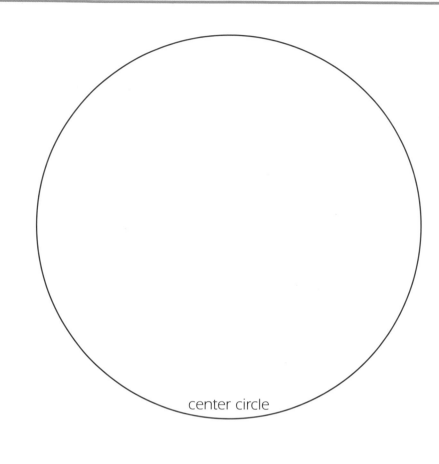
center circle

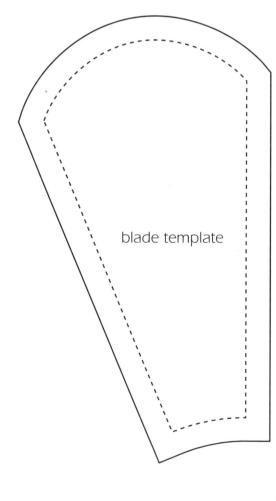
blade template

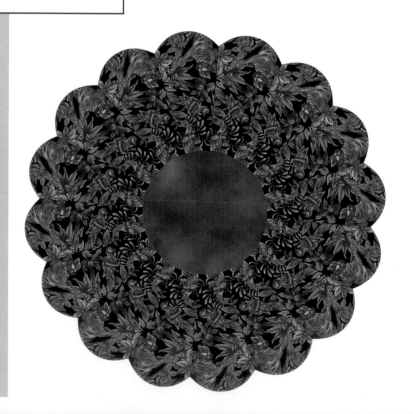

Dresden Plates of Distinction *Sharon Stroud*

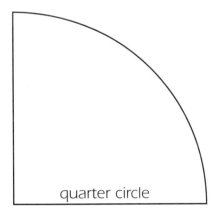

quarter circle

half circle

A Bit of "Fine China"

54" x 74". Joyce Janowski of Auburn, New York, pieced and appliquéd this quilt. Each plate contains a number of different motifs, making the most of this beautiful floral print. Machine quilted by Terry Simmons, Auburn, New York.

53½" x 73½". Gina Castro of Skaneateles, New York, used this large-scale tropical fabric to best advantage. Each plate is a visual feast for the eyes. Machine quilted by Terry Simmons, Auburn, New York.

DINNER IN PARADISE

FINE CHINA

58" x 78". Cathy Bush of Skaneateles, New York, used a border print fabric for her blades. The stripes add a swirling motion, while the paisley-like motifs add a touch of elegance. Machine quilted by Terry Simmons, Auburn, New York.

54" x 74". Sandy Forrest of Hector, New York, used a smaller-scale print to good advantage. The motifs are diverse but subtle, drawing the eye into each plate. Machine quilted by Terry Simmons, Auburn, New York.

WHEN THIS YOU SEE, REMEMBER ME

Dresden Plates of Distinction   *Sharon Stroud*

P & B CHALLENGE

21" x 21". I made this quilt for a local shop's P & B Challenge. I'm proud to say that it got an honorable mention! Notice that there are no center circles on these half plates. Hand quilted by the author.

56" x 56". Anita Shackelford of Bucyrus, Ohio, appliquéd all her partial plates directly to the background, using a center only on the full plate. This makes the quilt appear more open. Compare this quilt to JACOBEAN GARDEN on page 37; same set, very different look. Hand and machine quilted by Anita.

HOME MADE CHRISTMAS

Resources

Ardco by QuiltSmith, Ltd.
252 Cedar Road
Poquoson, VA 23662
Phone: 800-982-7326
Website: ardcotemplates.com
Window-style metal template DPW-14C

The Stencil Company
28 Castlewood Drive
Cheektowaga, NY 14227
Phone: 716-656-9430
Website: quiltingstencils.com
Quilting stencils for backgrounds and borders

Thimble Works
PO Box 462
Bucyrus, OH 44820
Website: thimbleworks.com
Mini Perfect Spiral marking tool, used on blades of
    SYMPHONY, page 25, JUNGLE, page 31, and BUGS, page
    22; on background of DALMATIANS, page 64
Mini fans and shells, used on SYMPHONY, page 25

Sharon Stroud
1155 Spring St. Ext.
Groton, NY 13073
Phone: 607-898-4639
Lectures and workshops

Sharon Stroud is an accomplished quiltmaker and teacher. A quilter since 1988, she started teaching part-time in 1991. Four years later, she quit her day job to devote more hours to teaching and quilting.

Dedicated to keeping hand skills alive, Sharon teaches hand appliqué, hand quilting, and hand piecing. She also teaches rotary cutting, precision machine piecing, binding, creative quilt labeling, and other techniques to give students a wide range of choices. She strives to keep the atmosphere in her classes light, believing that students learn more when they are having fun. With high standards for her own work, she encourages students to achieve their personal quilting goals. Students have nominated her five times for the Quilt Teacher of the Year Award, sponsored by *The Professional Quilter.*

Sharon's quilts have been successfully shown at state and national levels. Many of her quilts have been shown in magazine articles. She is a member of the American Quilter's Society, The Appliqué Society, and the National Quilting Association. She has served as a juror at several national shows, and is a quilt show committee member for Quilts=Art=Quilts at the Schweinfurth Memorial Art Center in Auburn, New York.

Sharon lives in Groton, New York, with her husband, Floyd, two cats, and a dog. Her husband is threatening to add at least one more room to the house, because he is certain that the two current sewing rooms will soon burst from the great amount of fabric, threads, finished and unfinished quilts, and just plain stuff in them!

This is only a small selection of the books available from the American Quilter's Society. AQS books are known worldwide for timely topics, clear writing, beautiful color photos, and accurate illustrations and patterns. The following books are available from your local bookseller, quilt shop, or public library.

#6001   US$21.95

#5848   US$19.95

#5336   US$22.95

#5855   US$22.95

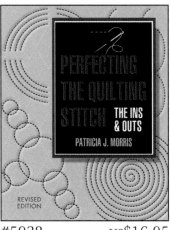

#5928   US$16.95

#5760   US$18.95

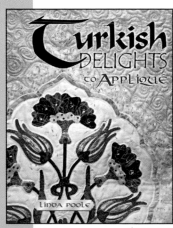

#6004   US$22.95

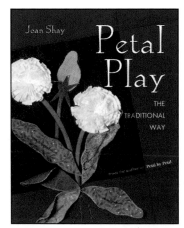

#5845   US$21.95

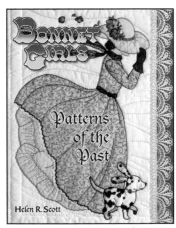

#5763   US$21.95

Look for these books nationally or call 1-800-626-5420